THE STARTUP SUCCESS PRIMER

SUCCESS MANTRAS FOR BUDDING FIRST GENERATION ENTREPRENEURS

D B PRABHU

Made with ♥ on the Notion Press Platform
www.notionpress.com

Dedicated to all those entrepreneurs who helped me to learn alongside them.

Contents

Acknowledgements

While working with first-generation entrepreneurs, I always thought that they needed a specific type of guidance. Standard management stuff is not for them. And neither are big motivational talks. So I have put together these 12 mantras for success.

This book is a result of the learnings from all the entrepreneurs whom I worked with, observed or simply met and interacted with. I thank all these entrepreneurial souls who enriched my experience.

I thank my school and college mates who helped me at various stages by responding to my surveys, suggesting title options and commenting on the cover design.

My family and office colleagues cannot be ignored for giving me the space needed. I sincerely thank them all.

And finally, most importantly, I thank the readers of my earlier books who gave me their valuable reviews and suggestions to improve my writing and its relevance.

Preface

The mission of my life is to help 100 first-generation entrepreneurs be successful in their business ventures. So I keep going to business meets, networking sessions, conferences etc. Some time back, at a business event, I met 4 different people.

There was a bright energetic college student. He was studying business management and he wanted to get into a business. I spoke to him for a while and I advised him to look for a job.

There was a mid-career professional with a fat salary at a big corporation. She was sick of her job and was toying with the idea of starting a business on her own with her massive savings. I suggested that she become an angel investor and continue her current career path.

The third person was a young professional in a software services company. He was in sales and was cracking big deals. He was on a roll. He had an idea of quitting and starting on his own in the same domain. I advised him to wait for a while, make a business plan and then come to me for further guidance.

The fourth one was a fresh graduate. He and a few of his friends wanted to explore the possibility of launching a startup. After talking to him for a while, I encouraged him and called him to my office. A few weeks later, he had registered his company and is now already in the business. He will grow eventually.

What made me give such diverse pieces of advice to all the above entities?

Entrepreneurship is not for everyone. 90% of startups fail in 5 years. And what more, while 90% of ventures fail, there are ventures 5 times that number which stayed as an idea or a dream that was never even tried.

Most aspiring entrepreneurs start with varying combinations of a big dream, a lot of passion, a lot of money, a great idea, a path-breaking innovation, brilliant founders, astounding academic credentials and so on.

And yet there are 90% failures. Why does this happen? What makes the 10% successful?

I think that **success or failure is determined right when the seeds of a venture are sowed.** Choosing the right seed and nurturing it the right way is completely in your hands!

These are heady days of speed when everyone wants astronomical valuations. But most of them are not ready for the long haul. Venture capitalists have also made a notion quite popular. Try quickly and fail fast rather than failing after a lot of investors' money has already been burnt away. I believe that it is **better to grow slow rather than fail fast.**

Entrepreneurship is not about valuation. It is about value. And creating value takes some time.

There are many books on the subject of entrepreneurship. All of them are great books but there is perhaps space for one more book - this one!

This book looks exactly at why 10% succeed and why the rest fail so that you can emulate what works and avoid the mistakes. And it is written specifically for 1st generation entrepreneurs by a 1st generation entrepreneur with first hand experiences of both successes and failures in his multiple ventures.

Is there a way to engineer your startup in a way that the odds of success are significantly high?

What can you do right in the beginning stages so that your chances of success increase significantly?

What factors should an entrepreneur consider before jumping onto the bandwagon?

And the most important, what delusions, illusions, and hallucinations he/she needs to come out of and the facts that he/she be actively conscious of before starting the most important journey of his or her life.

I have used some cases that I have seen closely. I could not name the companies or the people for obvious reasons. Some of the readers may be able to connect the dots and do their guesswork, but what is more important is the learning from these stories.

I have compiled these learnings into 12 key mantras for you to work on before you get into a business. But remember, knowing a mantra is not good enough. You need to activate it. And the way to do that is to ponder upon the questions presented after each of the stories and their analysis. Work diligently on them and the 12 mantras will guide you through the initial pre-startup days to create an unfair advantage in your favour.

I look forward to including your success story in one of my future books!

CHAPTER ONE

Mantra One

Get Your Reasons Right And Clear

Rajesh was a Director of Sales at a multinational software company. He is absolutely brilliant, a University gold medalist, a go-getter, and a high-performance man. After about 12 years in a series of corporate jobs, he was at the peak of his career. High back chair, corner cabin, chauffeur-driven car, personal assistant, a few managers reporting to him and all that. He led a sales team of more than 200 people across the country and all of them worked hard to beat their targets consistently and took home hefty salaries and even fatter bonuses. But Rajesh was not happy.

And it showed. The handsome person that he once was now sported a paunch, double chin, puffy eyes and a receding hairline. This guy who once regularly played tennis and football was now complaining about breathlessness and trouble with joints.

One Saturday evening, when we met for a casual dinner, Rajesh said, "Buddy, suggest me a great business to start. I am sick of working for someone else. I can spare the same effort for myself and be much wealthier!"

As an entrepreneurial mentor, he wanted me to help him set up a venture of his own. I simply took it as frustrated banter and we moved on to other subjects. I did not think he was serious at all.

I came to know a little later that Rajesh had quit his job and started a software services business of his own. Some of his big clients from his old company had moved their accounts to Rajesh. So it was a great start. I was a bit surprised but wished him luck anyway. 20 months later, Rajesh had closed down the business with heavy losses.

This time I wasn't surprised at all. I just felt bad for his loss. But it was much more than financial losses. For Rajesh, it was a heartbreak. After folding up the business, he started behaving weird.

He used to leave home in the morning and come back at night. But no one knew where he was and what he was doing. He was avoiding his clients, employees, old friends, and even his family. He had become a loner. I came to know that he was looking for a job. I tried to call him a couple of times to see whether I could be of any help. But he did not receive the calls.

Then, one fine day he suddenly appeared at my office. He was really desperate and completely broke. We talked about a few possible job openings for him. I assured him, I will sniff out something for him. One of my clients who was getting in the growth stage of his business seemed to be interested in hiring him. (Eventually, he did. And both Rajesh and his employer are very happy now!)

Then, as things moved to other topics I asked about his business and why things went wrong. After all, Rajesh was a capable person.

He just said, "I ran out of money."

Rajesh had paying customers from day one. But he still ran out of money. He attributed it to the high cost structures that he built up in anticipation of funding. He said he misjudged and mismanaged his finances.

Of course, that was one of the reasons for closing down. And it was perhaps a prudent decision to close and cut down his losses before they became any bigger. But losing money was just a visible result. It was the effect of underlying root causes.

These reasons were hidden in the remark that he had made over dinner.

Think about it. There are multiple subtle aspects in that remark. And if you are making similar statements, beware!

There are many things working at your subconscious level. You hold certain beliefs and nurture them to justify your words or opinions.

One, you believe that you will be successful in business.

Two, you believe that you will be happier than if you were in a job.

Three, you believe that you 'slog' in a job and 'work' in a business.

Four, you believe that 'you' and 'your business' are the same.

Five, you believe that you will not be answerable to anyone.

Well, just swallow this bitter pill right in the beginning.

There is no guarantee that you will be successful in your venture. No one can guarantee that. Besides, if you are an aspiring entrepreneur as per the expected reader profile for this book, there is no track record to prove anything. So as of now, it is only a wishful dream.

But if you are a successful professional like Rajesh, with some great deals or some marquee projects under your belt, you may have the same confidence of being successful and doing better in your own business. But delivering a great performance as an employed professional is a completely different ball game than being successful in business.

So do not connect your previous success to your future. It's a common disclaimer in any investment prospectus. "Past performance does not guarantee future returns". It is 100% applicable when it comes to starting on your own and writing your success story.

If you are not happy in your current job, there is no guarantee that you will be happy in your own business as well unless you know the reasons for your unhappiness. If you are not clear about why you are unhappy, chances are good that you will stay that way irrespective of what you do. Happiness is a state of mind. If you are unhappy in your job for the right reasons such as a mismatch between your job profile and your interests or your passion lies in something else, perhaps you may do well to quit. But if it is for all the wrong reasons like lower pay, too much work, a tough boss, or tougher customers, you will be worse off in your new venture.

And if you thought that in your own business, you would be the boss and have people working for you, and so you will do only the stuff that interests you, you are in for a rude shock. If it's your own business, you will need to slog more. The buck stops at you. You can afford to stick to your work profile in a job. But as an entrepreneur, your portfolio is the biggest!

The business that you set up is a different entity. "You" are not "the business". So your notion of working for yourself is completely wrong. You are still working for a company. This company is different from you. Just that you happen to own it. But you and your company are two different entities. Unless you understand this, it can cause a lot of heartburn for you later.

And if you feel that you are not answerable to anyone, brace yourself. You are answerable to everyone around you. You are answerable to your customers. You are answerable to your vendors. You are answerable to your employees. You are answerable to investors. You are answerable to the Government. You are answerable to the media. You are answerable to your family. You are answerable to everyone connected to your business in any way.

Rajesh started his entrepreneurial journey for the wrong reasons with the wrong beliefs. His main idea was to gain personal freedom. He believed he would be able to lead a relaxed life once he started his own business. He thought that after getting a few marquee clients, he would be able to raise money easily. He believed that he could hire people to substitute for him. He had seen too many of these "run your business on autopilot" webinars.

He learned the hard way that autopiloting is for a plane that is already cruising very well. Not when it takes off. Not before it reaches a cruising altitude.

So get your reasons right. That is the first step.

There are many things that you would have heard. Align with your passion, Find your Ikigai, Have a larger cause, and so on. All of that is great. But you don't need to make it so complex. Keep it simple. Take the quiz below.

Why do you want to start a business?

What is your personal goal?

How will starting this business help in achieving that goal?

What will happen if you achieve this goal?

What will happen if you don't achieve it?

And be absolutely true to yourself.

Many people make the mistake of trying to "get" these answers right. They try to justify their thoughts. But that would defeat the purpose of this exercise. The aim is not to get correct answers. The aim is to seek true answers and check whether they are worth dying for.

For example, most people are shy of saying that money is their motive. There is nothing wrong with money. How do you run a business without making money? So if money is a motive, so be it. However sinister it may seem to you, write your real motive. You may ask yourself again and again, 'Oh, is it?" or, "Do I really want this?"

A lot of times you feel you want something today. Ask yourself, once I get it, will I still want it more? Or will I want this same thing 10 years down the line? That should give you an idea about what will make you really happy.

Look, You are the most important person. If you are getting into a business, it should be for your own benefit in the first place. You can add the social angle later. All of it can happen after the business is successful...after you make a lot of money...after you do not need to work for money anymore.

Be clear about your needs, wants, and aspirational goals. Once they are all fulfilled, you will be able to focus on your self-realisation and self-actualization stuff. Do not start with that. Those will be the fruits of your hard labour. In the Bhagavad Gita, Lord Krishna urges you to focus on your efforts. Thinking too much about the results only leads to hallucinating.

Ensure that you do not have any illusions about yourself, your goals, or your expectations about the business. Just focus on the 5 questions. Answer the question without thinking about anything else other than that particular question in your context. I repeat, in "your context" alone.

To test whether your belief is justified or an illusion, simply ask someone you trust whether he/she sees it the same way. Or better still, hire a professional mentor.

One major trait of an entrepreneur is to ask for help. So do not hesitate to ask. You will be surprised how many people are willing to help.

CHAPTER TWO

Mantra Two

Analyse Yourself Critically

I am connected with a few incubation centres. So, I keep talking to many wannabe entrepreneurs.

In one of such interactions, I met Suresh. He was a bright engineering student and was a consistent academic performer. He was pursuing Civil Engineering at a highly reputed institute. He wanted to get into the food business.

It often surprises me that many people from core technical backgrounds want to get into unrelated businesses! While there is nothing wrong with that, I always think that it may be ideal that they build a business around their core area of expertise. I myself run a business outside of my core expertise. After all these years I have now gathered the relevant skills. But I believe that if I had some prior grounding in academics and work experience, my learning curve could have gone down and I may have done better.

Coming back to Suresh's story, his reasons were that he was quite passionate about food, he loved experimenting with food and he loved feeding people. Besides, he said, "Food is one of the few all-season, crisis-proof, money-making businesses."

I talked to Suresh and asked him what made him feel that he would be successful. And he shared with me his logic. All of the points were perfectly valid and it seemed he had studied the business well. He further gave me some success stories of his friends.

"My neighbour started a tiffin business during the pandemic. Now he is quitting his job. My cousin's friend started a baking business. Now she is setting up a retail outlet for cakes and pastries. There are so many of them. Everyone in the food business is successful!." But clearly, he was not just overly influenced by their success.

He had a solid business plan in mind. He had identified his startup team. They had worked out the bootstrapping for initial funding. He had also listed down a couple of contacts who would be willing to fund him if he needed more money. He was keen on a multi-cuisine exotic food restaurant. He was himself very good at some amazing Lebanese and Turkish cuisine. Apart from himself, he had identified the source for his chefs and he was pretty sure he would have a great business once the word spread.

Suresh turned down a decent pre-placement offer from a reputed engineering projects company. He and three of his friends borrowed money from their parents and set the project on track. They hired a reasonably big place at a decent location, put together some thematic furniture, started marketing aggressively on social media, tied up with Zomato and Swiggy and so on.

They had a really good marketing engine and they had decent bookings both for fine dining as well as takeaways in the opening week. They got raving reviews about the food quality, ambience, and overall dining experience. Over the next couple of months, the business blossomed. With planned media coverage, their fame spread. The team worked hard. Their dining room was always full. They were making good money and Suresh started thinking about expansion. And all this was within less than a year of starting!

But he had a dilemma. He had to choose between moving to a new larger place or starting multiple outlets. Starting in a new place would mean risking the loss of existing neighbourhood customers. Also, even in the new bigger place, they would still be addressing a relatively small neighbourhood. The 4 partners decided to start 3 additional outlets. That way, they would be able to multiply rather than add their business revenues!

So they sought assistance from some bankers and with a combination of debt and their cash reserves, they launched 3 brand new outlets with a major media blitz.

Before the 3rd anniversary, all 4 outlets were closed.

Why did this happen?

They were doing excellent in the beginning. What went wrong?

Suresh was a great chef. His 3 other partners were good at marketing, operations and finance respectively. Collectively they were a great team. But individually, they were incomplete. When they ran a single outlet, their skills converged to deliver a tremendous value to the business.

They were sure they would deliver the same value to all the 4 outlets. Anyways remote work was possible through technology.

Once the outlets were live, in the first few days, they all did well. The purchase was always central in order to maintain the quality and get good discounts. The recipes were standardised and Suresh trained the chefs himself. The prices were standardised and finance was all handled centrally.

But they miscalculated the softer problems of running a solo show each.

When it was a single outlet, all 4 of them had enough time to give a personal touch to every customer including their web delivery customers. The service staff was also constantly under vigilance and got continuous tips informally for improvement. All that made the guest feel special. People came to their outlet for the experience.

The moment they split into 4 outlets, they were unable to give the same amount of personal attention. The workload suddenly multiplied by 4 for each of them. Suresh was too busy training and monitoring chefs at all 4 outlets. The new cuisine development time was reduced. Financial management took up thrice the time. Though procurement was central for quality standardisation, controlling and ensuring quality at the delivery point took up too much time. The staff training time seemed to vanish.

The guy with finance expertise at one outlet was completely occupied because he now had to maintain 4 separate finance centres as well as reconcile all of them into "a single version of truth"! The guy with operations expertise could not optimise and monitor operations at all the outlets simultaneously. Processes at the other outlets slowly fell out of sync. The guy with marketing expertise was able to deliver well. But at the cost of managing his own outlet

As a result, the quality of customer experience started dwindling. The staff motivation level started going down. Footfalls started decreasing. Along with it, revenue started falling. To cope with dipping finances, they had to cut some expenditures. This resulted in further deterioration in customer experience. Revenues decreased, costs went up and there was a debt to pay. All of it triggered a downward spiral.

The 4 partners were individually great performers. Each one was a functional champion. But none of them was a good leader. But when they had to sail completely on their own, they could not hold the ship. They simply did not have entrepreneurial skills.

Entrepreneurship is not about having great functional skills yourself. And yet, at the same time, to be an entrepreneur you need certain stuff.

And the most important of that is knowing yourself well. It is mandatory that you do a critical assessment of yourself. It is popularly called SWOT analysis. Strengths, Weaknesses, Opportunities and Threats. But we do not need to make it so complex at this stage.

As of now, it is just about you. We want to see whether you are good enough as an entrepreneur. So list out your strengths and weaknesses as a person.

Many people make a mistake here. They list the strengths and weaknesses of their proposed business. You need to understand that you and your business are different. We are trying to see if you are good enough. Not whether the business is good or bad. For that, there are different methods.

Once you know these strengths and weaknesses, think about whether any of your weaknesses can be overcome. For example, you may have a weakness in understanding finance. Can you undergo a short finance course and equip yourself enough?

And there may be certain weaknesses that you may simply not be able to overcome. Or maybe, the cost and time involved in overcoming them are unreasonably high. For example, you may not know the technical skills core to your business. You can decide to outsource this skill in some other fashion. In Suresh's case, he sourced these functional skills through his cofounders.

Most great entrepreneurs do not have all the necessary strengths to start and run a business. They may have a few. But their biggest skill is that they are great leaders. They communicate phenomenally well. They inspire people. They instil trust and confidence. They have charisma. And they transfer their passion to their team!

Another important soft skill is 'business sense'. You need to have open eyes and ears and an "always-on" calculative mind working together. You observe. You map trends. You analyse. And you predict. Based on these predictions you make calculated decisions. All the much-touted risk-taking traits of entrepreneurs are based on this ability to make calculated decisions.

One of the things that an entrepreneur must be able to do is to gather all the resources required for the business - the 3 M - money, material and men. (The word "Men" is gender agnostic here!). It is relatively easy to acquire money and material. But getting the right men (people) and amalgamating them into a homogenous team is a phenomenal task.

So ask yourself these questions.

What are the core skills needed for my business?

Am I sufficiently skilled in the core areas of my business? If not, can I get the right people who are? How am I going to get them?

If I get these people, am I good at handling them?

Am I a good observer? A good listener? A good storyteller?

Can I lead a team? Can I get the team to do things?

And when it comes to getting a team to do things, there are many characteristics you need to have or inculcate within yourself.

Let us do a small exercise.

List down some essential characteristics of some great business leaders you know.

Check how many of these traits are already there in you.

Verify your assumption by asking a close friend.

Check whether it is possible to develop the rest of the traits.

Make a plan for developing these traits.

Many times, people find it difficult to do this exercise on their own without a bias. Usually, you cannot see all the sides of your own persona. A third party view is useful. A good friend who has the courage to point out your flaws is a great asset in this situation. You may seek professional assistance as well.

By the way, Suresh and his friends are now comfortable in their respective jobs. They took up post-graduation in their respective disciplines and got good campus placements. Their failed venture and the lessons learnt helped them tremendously in securing high profile jobs!

Entrepreneurial experience is never wasted!

CHAPTER THREE

Mantra Three

Know Your Business

Do you know exactly what your business is?

This seems to be a very silly question to ask an aspiring entrepreneur. But the number of times that I have got blank stares, together with those when I got some astoundingly unrealistic answers, is so surprising that I had to include this as one of the most important mantras before you start.

I was at an exhibition for recyclers where we were displaying our machinery and talking about our consulting services. We had a visitor named Anand. Anand wore the look of a simple but purposeful guy. He wanted to get into the business of recycling electronic waste.

As usual, I asked Anand about his background, his reasons for getting into business, and probed him more about his interest in the e-waste business. He didn't know much, but he seemed to be quite grounded in this thinking. At the end of the conversation, we built decent mutual respect.

Anand was a young graduate. He had completed a basic bachelor's degree and had been hunting for a job for a long time. He couldn't get something that matched his liking. The offers that he got were either too low or had some ridiculous demands. Naturally, he was jobless for quite some time. That's when he started thinking about doing something on his own and being a job creator rather than a job seeker.

While this seems to be the case of "the accidental entrepreneur", you may be surprised to know that the number of entrepreneurs who were "forced into entrepreneurship" because they could not get a decent job is quite high! In fact, not being able to get a job is one of the leading motivations for people turning to entrepreneurship!

And their proportion among successful businessmen is also quite high! The most famous example that comes to my mind is that of Jack Ma. But there are many not so famous like him.

Back to Anand, he had no money and no backing at all. He came from a very simple middle-class family. No one in his family had ventured into business. Getting a job and sticking to it for a lifetime was what his elders had always done. He had no academic qualifications for any business whatsoever.

And yet, for some reason, I did not feel like discouraging him. I usually do that a lot. Of 10 people who express interest in any kind of business, I usually dissuade 7 or 8. In many cases, people are simply not ready to jump into an entrepreneurial role. I discourage such people. It is much better than having heartburn and cash loss later.

In the case of Anand, I made an exception. But though I did not dissuade him, I did not encourage him either. Somehow, I thought he could be successful. But I had no supporting evidence.

Over the next 6 to 8 months, Anand was out of my direct contact. But he was visible in many online recycling forums, discussions, events etc. One fine day, he bought our entry-level machinery.

It generally does not happen that way with our business. First customers sign up for consulting and then eventually they go for the machinery. Anand didn't have the money to invest in consulting. So he invested his time and efforts instead.

Over the next 2 years, we were in casual touch. He had still not signed up for any consulting, but he did seek some guidance from time to time. Through the nature and quality of his questions, I knew that he was doing well.

After 2 years, Anand was ready for expansion. He came back and bought from us a new set of machinery 4 times the capacity. And this time he signed up for advanced consulting services too.

He now had a decent sized team working for him. He was clocking a turnover of about 4 crores and he was considering a 10x growth in 5 years. He had also roped in an investor for realizing this growth.

I was pleasantly surprised. How can this happen? A simple, not so qualified, middle-class person without any entrepreneurial background gets into business. That too because he can't get a decent job. And he builds the business all on his own and makes it a success!

Let me tell you at this point, e-Waste recycling is not an easy business at all. It is a very challenging but very promising business if you get your game right. And getting it right is extremely challenging for a 1st generation, barely educated, investment starved person.

When I asked him later about it, he laughed and said, "I studied the business. And I grew it one ton at a time, in your language, one step at a time."

One ton at a time! That was so perfect!

Anand was successful purely because he put his head down and went to work on the field. He did his own research. He validated it through seminars, events, etc and filtered out the right kind of intelligence relevant to him.

He started small. He did one simple pass-through transaction first. He found a supplier, he found a buyer and brokered a deal. He repeated it over and over. In each transaction, he learnt. He learnt the science of finding his potential scrap suppliers. He learnt the knack of procurement. He learnt the art of negotiating with his potential buyers.

Also, in the meantime, he learnt recycling processes in principle. He understood the system. He understood the legal framework. And he applied his mind to create his own trademark processes.

He appointed a few people and trained them in specific functions. His business model slowly evolved from brokering sporadic transactions to an organized e-waste recycling company. He created his own supply chain for meeting the monthly volume of procurement.

That is when he came and bought his first set of machinery from us. He became a formally registered recycler and his business only grew. He consolidated it. He tested his forecasts over and over till he was reasonably confident.

Within 2 years he had a reasonably stable business and his hunger for growth started surfacing. But he was also aware that beyond a point he couldn't run on his own. He needed external funding. He needed additional expertise if he had to convert his small business into a well-structured enterprise. That's when he roped in an investor and hired us as his consultant.

That's exactly how you build a business. Step by step. Today in the world of steep valuations and meteoric growth, the age-old wisdom of consolidating your foundations is forsaken. That's dangerous in the long run. That is precisely the reason behind high failure rates in startups.

Consolidation happens only when you acquire deep knowledge about your business. You must know it in and out. You have to go through ups and downs. You have to know how to tame the beast of growth and also how to protect the business in bad times.

Anand did not just study and discover the business mechanics through a practical hands-on learning process, but more importantly, he understood the crux of the business, what his business was about.

One thing that really stuck in my mind was what Anand told me once. "I am not in the recycling business. I am in the business of value-added matchmaking. I have to identify the ever-changing market needs of both the procurement side and the sales side. I have to bridge the gaps between both sides by adding appropriate value to the scrap."

That means a lot. But explaining it in detail will mean diverting ourselves into understanding the e-waste business. That is not our agenda as of now.

What is critical here is to know the business so well that you exactly know why you are doing what you are doing.

It is often surprising that people conduct business "out of habit". There is a practice of doing certain things and they keep doing it over and over without thinking of any value addition. That way businesses live. But they do not thrive.

As an entrepreneur, especially as a startup, you must know where, when, what and how much value you add exactly. Else you get reduced to a transacting merchant.

Many times these areas of value addition are considered as functional processes. Many times they are simply cast in stone. But value is a dynamic thing. Value demanded and value delivered both keep changing from time to time. If you are able to provide the right balance between demanded value and the perception of the delivered value, you grow. And that's what I mean by saying, do you know your business?

So how do you know this? What does it mean to you? And isn't it all related to 'after you start the business?'

Well, no. Business understanding and redefinition is a continuous process. But, it is of most critical importance before you start your business planning.

Let us answer the following questions.

Who could be your customers? What will drive them to work with you?

Who could be your suppliers? What will drive them to work with you?

What value will you exactly provide to your customers and suppliers?

How are you going to create/deliver this value?

How will your customers and suppliers perceive your delivered value?

Remember, the real business of an entrepreneur is to create value for customers. If you can answer the above questions, you would understand your real business very well.

Anand's story highlights how he tried to understand the business before he started, how he learned in his startup phase and how he kept learning as he stabilized. At a point when he knew he couldn't learn on his own anymore, he hired consultants.

Today, though we provide a lot of consulting services to Anand, he is one of my mentors too!

CHAPTER FOUR

Mantra Four

Get A Crack Team

Here are 3 separate stories.

Swati and I were attending a seminar about financial freedom when we first met. We ended up talking about our businesses during the breaks.

Swati was working with a famous international fashion designer. But she now wanted to start on her own.

I could make out that she was a supremely confident young lady. She was a qualified commercial artist and had an impressive portfolio of very creative designs. She had a lot of contacts within the fashion industry and was well connected to fabric suppliers, models, embroiders, textile printers, tailors and so on.

She had decent financial backing from her family too. So starting on her own was apparently the most natural course for her. She had all the necessary ingredients in place.

She was quite charged up by virtue of her talent, her connections and of course the seminar that talked so much about achieving financial freedom through entrepreneurship.

Very soon, I was invited to a grand opening ceremony of her design boutique. She had a couple of celebrities at the event and had a very impressive display of her designs. She had a couple of assistants who worked under her direction. The business launch was a ringing success.

Her business did very well and she soon started thinking about expansion. She needed extra funding for that. She wanted to grow the business multifold and the investment needed could only be availed through a venture capitalist. The amount of debt she could raise was not going to be sufficient.

She has been trying to get funding for expansion for quite some time now. She is finding it tough to convince investors despite her great negotiation skills and despite having a decently profitable outlet.

At another event, I met Kajal. She had a strong techno-commercial grounding thanks to her graduation from a renowned engineering college and a management degree from a premium institution. She had been toying with the idea of setting up a mobile software apps company. She even had the prototypes ready.

She had associates from her alma mater as cofounders and each one of them had clearly cut out jobs. Kajal focused on strategic directions and was the technical evangelist. Komal, her MBA friend was their marketing head. Supreet was another one from her engineering college and he was in charge of product development. She had already identified someone to onboard for handling the marketing and sales. And she was contemplating outsourcing the other services such as financial services and HR.

There was a phenomenal value proposition in the apps that Kajal and her team had created. They were meant for boosting the productivity of small and midsize companies who could not afford to invest in complex high cost solutions. The revenue model was based on an affordable annual subscription. It was a solid business plan.

However, she just did not have the financial muscle. Kajal and her team needed big money for two things - hiring developers to be able to take the prototype to production and to market the products. Her individual financial status was not very great to enable the venture. With her background getting a sizeable institutional business loan was not possible. She had no option but to look for an investor.

I knew someone who invested in technology companies and suggested that she meet him. A few months later, a deal was done and Kajal launched her company with a live online worldwide product launch attended by over 20,000 small and mid-size companies.

In a third situation, I met Prashant. He also had an app-based business in mind. He was starting afresh along with his engineering batchmates. All of them were super smart hardcore techies with excellent academic pedigree.

The product was for making digital payments easier and safer for all. They had a prototype and a decent product roadmap in place. Very strong security features, multilingual capabilities, ease of use, multi-platform compatibility and loyalty enhancement features were their strong points.

They showcased their product prototype to a couple of large FMCG companies and some showed interest in trying out their beta version. Since Prashant and his team were all rookies, they bootstrapped their venture and started the development.

But they knew that to convert the beta into a complete market-tested product, they had to get financial backing. Their natural choice for funding was the same companies who had showed interest in the pilot. They were quite confident that they would be able to get advances from these companies.

It turned out that they did get a good amount of money but they knew they would soon run out of it. The product was far too complicated than they had anticipated earlier. Besides, there were other costs to meet such as salaries, rent, technology services and so on.

They have been talking to quite a few investors for a long time now. Their discussion goes a few steps ahead on a very positive note before ultimately fizzling out. This is a bit of a nasty surprise for the team.

In all the 3 cases above, the business models are solid, the products are good, the market exists and they all have paying customers. Why is it that one of them got funding easily and the rest are struggling to get it?

The key lies in the team that they had or did not have. It is that important. Investors always look at your team. They know that the success of a business is dependent on the quality of the team.

So what kind of team do you need? And what kind of team do you have? What are the gaps and how can you fill them?

In Kajal's case, clearly, she did not have a marketing person on board. Neither did she have HR and finance people. But she was clear about what she was going to do to fill those gaps.

Swati did not have a team. She was a great leader herself. But the rest of the team did not have those skills. One key responsibility of a leader is to create new leaders under herself. That way you can delegate your work. If you cant delegate you cant take on new responsibilities. If you as a business head cant take on new responsibilities, there is no way your business can grow beyond a point.

In the case of Prashant, he had a team. But the team was full of all techies. There was no management expertise. Businesses cant run with technical knowledge alone. You need managerial and administrative skills. Most small entrepreneurs are technocrats or domain experts. You need a sharp management team to scale up.

Precisely due to this difference, investors looked at these scenarios differently.

The point to highlight is that if you want to start a business, you can very much do it yourself. But if you want to make it big, if you want to sustain for the longer term, if you want to keep pace with the market, you need a team. You cant do it all alone.

So how do you get this team? Should you have multiple founders? Should you simply go the good old way of hiring the right people? Should you outsource some functions?

In all the 3 cases, the considerations are different. Especially if you are a startup, you are usually broke. You can't afford to hire the required talent. So you tend to find co-founders or partners. You sell your dream to them. You convince them about the business potential and entice them to work with you and invest their time and efforts in anticipation of rich rewards.

However, if people simply come together for the rewards, such teams usually do not perform and the business does not last long. For a solid business team, your team members need to share your vision, passion and purpose. That is a bigger reward than the money for these people. Such teams can create wonders.

But at the same time, this also may mean sharing equity. That can be a big cost over time. Equity is an expensive asset to give away. So if you are planning to get your team members in this manner you need to be extra careful.

An easier way is to simply hire the required talent. But that costs money from day one. However, it is the best option in the long run. You do not dilute your equity and neither do you need to worry about what to do with someone who doesn't perform. In the long term, this is the cheapest option.

But it is not easy to hire talented people for a startup without paying handsome salaries. For peanuts, you get only monkeys. They will keep jumping from one place to another. For stable performers, you need to pay them well. The question is can you afford it at the beginning of your venture?

Outsourcing some functions is always an option. Depending on your business, there will always be a few functions that are not core to the business. These can be surely outsourced. This is not the cheapest, but perhaps the most cost-effective HR strategy.

Do it whichever way you like, but get yourself a crack team.

Finally, how do you scrutinize people for different roles in the team?

Check their interests, passion, ambition, personal and financial background, skills, knowledge and overall what they will contribute to the business. Be also very candid to set their expectations right. Whether you are hiring an employee or inducting a partner, make sure that you give them complete clarity about their role.

Let us answer these questions.

What kind of skills do you need for running the business?

Among the people you know very well, can you spot these skills? How can you attract these people to work with you?

What roles are you trying to fill up? Define the role and the responsibilities clearly.

What is the value that you expect this role to deliver to the business?

What are your compensation models in order of preference? Can you list them role-wise?

These answers are a bit tough to answer in one sitting. Working along with a professional consultant is the best way to tackle this part. Ultimately the founding team writes the fortunes of the business.

CHAPTER FIVE

Mantra Five

Plan Your Finances

I met an interesting young gentleman at the airport quite accidentally. We were both sitting on adjacent chairs in the waiting lounge. He was reading a book titled something like how to start a multi-million dollar business. Naturally, I was interested in this person. (I don't remember the exact book title or the author. But that's not the point anyway.)

After a while, he kept the book down, and I took the opportunity to start a conversation. I gave him my digital business card which also gave him the links to download some of my ebooks. On knowing about me, he opened up quite a bit.

His name was Ravi. He was ambitious and highly qualified. He had done his engineering from a premier institute and then his MBA from yet another institute of prestige. He was currently working at a decent position in a large MNC.

He was also enrolled with a certain business coach who was very good at inspiring his students to visualize aspirational goals. And Ravi being decently qualified, very ambitious and coming from a reasonably well to do family, naturally was completely convinced that he should start on his own.

He had already started a company with his wife as the second shareholder. The company was currently bootstrapped from their own money. It was in the domain of renewable energy. He had a deep technical understanding of the domain thanks to his electrical engineering degree. And given the market demand for alternate energy sources, it was an overall good fit.

When I asked him more, I came to know that he was planning to raise the rest of the money from family and friends. He was thinking of inviting them to be minority equity holders. But they would be just passive investors. He would be hiring a team of talented professionals and leading the team himself as a CEO.

The salaries of these highly talented people including himself would come from the investor's money. He already had a few people who had committed about a crore of Rupees each for minor stakes. The money was yet to come through.

I asked him three simple questions out of curiosity.

How did you arrive at the equity sharing formula?

Are they aware of the projected cash flow? In other words, have you shown them how their money will be deployed?

What is the exit plan for them?

He said he had given them an idea about the profitability and they have committed their investment considering the large potential to grow in the long run. And they did not intend to exit at all. But it was not convincing enough to me.

Nevertheless, he was confident that he will be able to get the required amount even if the currently committed potential investors were to withdraw.

This event happened more than 3 years ago. Ravi's company is still on paper and Ravi is still in his job.

Now think about it.

Was the business bad? Not at all! Renewable energy is definitely a promising business.

Was Ravi incapable of running the show? Not really. He had all the required credentials. He had also defined the hiring roles for the actual execution. He had spoken to an HR consultant for these roles and the consultant had assured him about getting the right people on board in a reasonable time frame of 3 months.

Was Ravi not resourceful enough to find investors? Or was he not able to invoke their interest? No. He was able to attract them. He was even able to convince them to agree to invest.

What he was unable to do was to get the guys to actually invest. He was able to invoke their interest in the project. But he was unable to answer the questions any investor may ask. He found them too tough to answer simply because he was not well prepared with his financial numbers.

He had made his excel sheets. He had figured out the expenses. He had figured out the potential profits. He had calculated annual returns. But he had no idea about his cash flow. He knew how much money he would need on day 1. But he did not know how much he would need on day 30 or day 100. He did not know his inventory cycles or production cycles.

Money, without the dimension of time, is of little value for planning and running a business successfully.

Many, rather most of your expenses are real-time. You cant meet present expenses through future cash flows. And for all you know, future cash is worth far less than the current cash.

So how do you get this money equation right?

Your expenses start on day zero. Your revenues start at some other time in the future. And depending on your business, the revenues may come in small regular instalments or in fewer but larger chunks.

Ravi's business was into renewable energy. Which meant he would get paid only after getting projects and successfully commissioning them. Till then his cash outflow would continue in form of salaries, rent, electricity bills, conveyance etc. It was very important for Ravi to know how long he could last without a single customer. It was also very important for him to know how long can he last with a single project. How many projects at what completion frequency and what margins will ensure that he will be able to meet his annual expenses. Ravi was not ready with all that.

So what should you do if you don't want to end up like Ravi?

Keep it simple. Just answer the following 5 questions and the jigsaw pieces will fall into place.

What are your fixed expenses whether you do any business or not?

What is the incremental expense that you incur for servicing a single order?

How frequently do you expect to get orders?

When do you expect to get paid? Are there any advances? Is there a payment window?

What is your capital investment? How long is it likely to last before you need a complete revamp?

The 1st 2 questions define your fixed and variable operating expenses. The 3rd and 4th questions define the inflow of your money.

Your fixed operating expenses will need to be paid from your capital and reserves. Generally this cost does not figure in the direct cost of production and therefore is sometimes missed by new entrepreneurs.

The variable operating expenses are incurred only when you have a project. This is a direct cost. Hence it will be always factored into your actual unit cost of production.

As long as your total operating expenses are completely covered by your earnings and if you are able to save some amount of money as your cash surplus, you should be fine.

Capital expenses are of secondary concern. You can recover them over a period of time through your cash surplus. Besides, capital expenses create assets that have a value and a defined lifetime. As long as your capital expense is recovered completely before the lifetime of the asset, you are good.

Ideally, your product costing should be a sum of your direct unit cost of production plus a part of your indirect costs, plus an appropriate part of your capex and your profit. You can decide the indirect operating cost apportioning based on the frequency of orders. The capex may also be apportioned similarly, but considering a slightly longer time horizon.

Another important aspect is how fast you can realize your payments. If your payment terms are in advance, it is great. But generally you will perhaps get a part in advance, a part on delivery and a small part in retention or a performance guarantee. Sometimes your customers will impose a standard payment clause of payment after a certain number of days from receipt of invoice. You will need to factor in that cost too.

The above aspects will ensure that you are afloat. If you need growth, you need to work on a single parameter of time.

How much can you sell in a defined timeframe? How fast can you produce a unit? If you can improve on both of the above against the parameter of time, you can improve your actual profits. Your indirect cost per unit will go down. Your capex apportioning per unit will also go down. This will result in a higher profit.

That is what investors will see. How much and how fast!

Ravi failed exactly here.

He has calculated expenses. But he had not figured out how much was fixed and how much was variable. It turned out that his fixed operating expenses were more than his variable operating expenses. Ideally, it should be the other way round.

Variable expenses are only incurred when you are fulfilling transactions. When you do transactions, you are making money. You don't mind incurring expenses against income. So try to convert more of your fixed operating expenses into variable ones. There are many ways you can do this. Outsourcing some of the mundane work is one example. A good process or operations consultant will be able to help you in this.

Investors don't mind their money being invested in getting more business or fulfilling orders faster or even creating capital assets. But, they would surely not be very kind if they see their money being used for funding fixed operating expenses.

And even if you are not taking any third party investments, all of that written here is applicable to you as well. In such a case, you are the investor yourself. You should always treat yourself as a separate entity than your business.

The business must take care of the investors' money. Whether the investors are third parties or whether you yourself have invested in the business. And you can take care of money when you understand its behaviour clearly.

Cash flows are therefore the most important criteria from a business planning perspective. Cash flow shows you how the money works. As long as it is smoothly flowing the business is healthy. The moment the cash flow stops or stagnates, the business starts developing ailment symptoms. That's why planning your finances is critical.

Financial planning is not only about where you will get the money from or where you will spend it. It is more about how much and when.

CHAPTER SIX

Mantra Six

Position Yourself Right

When you think about a business, it is critical that you know your customers very well. Based on your understanding of how they think and act, what excites them, what turns them off, and so on, you have to create a space for yourself in the marketplace. You need to present yourself in a way that resonates with their persona. This is exactly what market positioning is all about. How effectively you do it and what position you choose to take makes a lot of difference.

I have a friend Rajeev. He is a very successful marketing consultant now. He has some great brands that he works for and he is doing very well for himself. But his journey was pretty interesting.

When Rajeev was doing his MBA he was convinced that marketing was his calling. This was one thing that excited him. He made a decision by the mid of his second year that he will make a career in marketing.

He could have been a hot candidate for any of the big consulting companies that came to his campus. In fact he already had a PPO from one of the big 5s. But he did not want to work for any of them. He had done his internship and he had noticed that in the big companies they really made the interns and the fresh candidates slog like crazy.

He was not a shirker and working long hours did not matter to him at all. Afterall, he had slogged days and nights to get into an IIT and then into an IIM and then to secure great grades at both places. But he thought that if he had to work hard, he may as well work harder for his own startup rather than for doing so for making the big ones bigger.

During his last two months in college, Rajeev started his consulting practice. He picked up the first assignment that he got within just a week of opening for business. It was a modest marketing job from a friend in the educational business. The job involved running a digital marketing campaign. This company was into advising and placing students in foreign universities. And the campaign was meant for generating quality leads.

He did not earn much if he were to count the cost of his time. But he had a very successful campaign and that earned him a few good references. One of the leads that was generated through his campaign became his next customer. He was a gym owner and he hired Rajeev for getting new customers for his gym. Again, it involved digital marketing and handling social media pages for the gym. He was responsible for creating the social media posts, monitor engagements, leverage them and lure them to visit the gym where the fitness consultant would convert this qualified lead into a sale.

The job paid well and soon there were other gyms seeking out Rajeev's services. His team grew. Revenues grew. But he was not happy. He was not doing any serious marketing stuff. He was simply creating digital assets and using them over and over with minor modifications. There was no quality work as a marketing consulting firm. His portfolio was simply getting clogged with "more of the same" and that too in an area that did not create much value. He was still at the bottom of the value chain in marketing despite his vision and abilities.

So one fine day after three odd years, he simply sold off this company to another larger digital content agency and walked out with very little to show. With the little money he made in the sale, he went on a vacation and came back with a fresh business plan.

He called his classmates, seniors, professors and friends for a business dinner. I was one of the invitees and I gladly grabbed this chance of meeting some very influential marketing brains. Rajeev pitched his idea of creating a company that would provide shared CMO services to mid size businesses who needed this position but could not attract the necessary talent. He persuaded them to join his company as part time project based associates. A few agreed to join, a few agreed to fund and thus was born Rajeev's new marketing services company.

He hired a small but elegant office in a business district. He started with 3 industry verticals for offering his services, found out the contacts of the owners, CEOs, CFOs, board members and other decision makers and the rest is history. Today after 6 years, Rajeev has a large swanky office, a battery of more than 50 management graduates working for him and a client base of more than 200 who have multi year contracts signed with him.

The lesson is clear. In his first venture, Rajeev did not portray his capabilities at all. He simply positioned himself as a marketing consultant and took whatever jobs he got. He did not create a position for himself. The market put him in a position that he accepted.

Now the problem with this was that since the market slotted him in that specific position, everything else including the nature of work, pay, people were all dictated by the market. There was no value addition. You just churned out high volumes of work like a commodities factory. While the business was doing well, Rajeev saw no great future. "Digital content company for personal care sector" became his whole identity and he was unable to break that image.

The important point is that he made a decision and acted upon it. He quit. It takes a lot of courage to quit from your own existing and profitably running business. When you sense a mistake, it is important that you correct it even though the cost of correction seems quite big. This cost is often, perhaps always, far lower than the loss that you would incur by rejecting the correction.

In his second avatar, Rajeev did not repeat his mistake. He knew what he was looking for. He positioned himself as a high profile serious consulting firm. He showcased the collective strength of his associates and he leveraged their contacts. He firmly said no to the mundane jobs and focused on those long term contracts for outsourced marketing services. He clearly positioned himself as a company selling CMOs!

Of course, in the process he struggled in the beginning, had some rejections, had to tweak his pricing models and so on. But those are the standard nuances of any new business. The key here is to position yourself in the manner that you want yourself to be known as, so that clients come to you with the perception that you want them to carry.

And even more important is to position yourself in front of the right market audience. Rajeev chose his target companies very well. He started with just 3 verticals to start with and a limited list of 90 carefully chosen companies. It turned out after 6 years that within this original target list of 90, eventually 86 became his customers!

Here is one more story. Yeshaswini and her team were on an anti plastic mission. So they developed a line of edible cutlery to replace single use plastic cutlery. They had major trouble finding a market. They had initially targeted environmental activist groups and tried using the online ecommerce portals. But the initial peak in response did not last long. After months of struggling, Yeshaswini realised that she needed to change her approach. In other words, she needed to get out of the position of an anti-plastic crusader.

She and her team researched the market once again. After several rounds of brainstorming on their research date, they identified a niche. They targeted banquets and resorts who hosted large functions. Yeshswini was earlier positioning her product to the customers as a green alternative to plastics. Now she changed her position and started selling the concept of having a green image to the banquet and resorts. She convinced them that an "eco-friendly" or environmentally responsible image will help their business. And then she came up with how she can help them to reinforce this image through a practical proof of offering edible cutlery to their guests. The resorts and banquets saw this not just as differentiation, but they also sensed the opportunity to charge a premium.

Instead of Yeshaswini telling the end customers about the benefits of her product, now the resorts and banquets positioned a whole new concept of eco-friendly events and how it enhanced their own image in the eyes of their invitees. In the process, they also highlighted to their customers how using edible cutlery shows care for the environment and simultaneously provides health benefits, as the product is made from natural ingredients and free from harmful chemicals. Additionally, most invitees were excited by the prospect of trying a new and innovative product, and the fun of enjoying a meal with cutlery that you can actually eat, and project their own image as environmentally sensitive.

These emotional appeals resonated with customers and the sale grew steadily over a few months. By appealing to the emotions of her customers and the customers' customers, Yeshswini created a stronger connection with them. She not only differentiated her product but also enabled her customers and their customers with a unique value proposition of their own!

So when you think about your own business, ask yourself these questions.

What is the perceived image that I want to create?

Which particular market segment sees value in this image?

In which all ways can my product or service reinforce this image?

Will this image be useful for selling more?

Am I showcasing the image to the right audience?

There are more things to it, but these are good questions to start with. Positioning is often a trial and error game. What seems correct to you may not seem so correct to someone else. Also, what is correct today, may not remain relevant tomorrow. So while creating a strong position, if you have to change it and take a different stance later, do not be afraid to do so. If you have a good product or service, just by positioning yourself right, you will be able to not only sell more, but also sell at a premium.

CHAPTER SEVEN

Mantra Seven

Choose Your Sales Strategy

Most of the startups that I have worked with had a great concept or a phenomenal product. They all talked about the concept or the product and how it will be a panacea for mankind. All of them were super confident that they are solving such a critical problem in their customer's lives that buyers will fall over each other to buy their product or service.

And they did talk about a sketchy production plan, a vague marketing plan and a hopeful funding plan. Almost all of them lacked a sales plan. The fundamental need of a business is revenue. And that comes from sales. All other functions are cash guzzlers. Sales is the only one that generates the cash for all of them. Needless to say, a sound sales strategy is super critical for a startup.

I know a brilliant commercial artist - Richa. She has a passion for jewellery design. Her passion led her to design and make some very innovative artificial jewellery. Her USP was that it was handmade jewellery. So her jewellery had the uniqueness of design and every piece was a designer piece.

After months of creative, passionate, hard work and of course some significant amount of capital, Richa launched her own store. She already had some great social media content and was a regular on Instagram, Facebook and Pinterest. Her designs had won some great number of likes and she had a fan base developed over a period of time. Based on her social media engagement, she was supremely confident of sales.

As it turned out, the day when the "Open for business" sign went up, she had quite a few friends walk in and the store saw a lot of footfalls and some sales as well. As the days progressed and the novelty wore off, the footfalls reduced and so did the sales.

Richa soon realised that she needed a robust marketing plan and effective sales strategies if she were to make more sales. She started by defining her target market and then focused on understanding their specific needs, budgets, buying patterns, etc.

She decided on 3 sales channels - her own shop, an online store and indirect sales through her customers in a MLM style.

She already had excellent relationships with her existing clients and her fan base as well. She went out of the way to provide special services to her clients by offering them a free bi-annual jewellery polishing service. Very smartly, in return she subtly took testimonials from them, took some stunning photographs and posted them on her social channels. She asked them to share it with their friends. She converted her customers into models and celebrities within their sphere of influence!

These same early clients now also became indirect channel partners for Richa. Richa offered them one piece of jewellery for every 5 units sold in the same price bracket. This helped her to reduce her inventory and improve her cash flow. The clients could also sell this extra piece and make extra money.

And further, Richa created an offer for all those who gave her reviews - including negative reviews. This boosted her social media traffic like anything. She diverted that traffic to the online store. Sales zoomed in no time.

Soon Richa moved to a bigger production facility where just the 1st few pieces were handmade and the rest were machine copies. The 1st few designer pieces were sold at a fat premium only through her physical store and the machine copies catered to the volumes drawn in by the online store.

As the next step, she partnered with local boutiques or gift shops to carry her jewellery. This gave her access to a new customer base. Additionally, partnering with established businesses helped her to enhance her brand and increase visibility for her products.

As of now, within seven years of starting her jewellery business, Richa is now thinking of diversifying into apparel as an extension. She is a busy successful entrepreneur!

In another case, Sushil was a finance minded IITian. He and his friends developed an AI based product for recommending stock market investments. The software took certain inputs from the user and based on the user profile, it recommended certain stocks. After the investments were made, it also advised buy, sell and hold positions. Furthermore, it had the option of automating transactions based on price thresholds.

Sushil and his co-developers had put in long hours to perfect the product and were eager to start selling. He was confident that it would disrupt the portfolio management industry. They decided to sell the software in a subscription model on the cloud.

However, they quickly realized that simply having a great product was not enough. They needed a strong sales strategy to get their product in front of the right customers and generate sales.

Being technology oriented, the team decided to take a data-driven approach to sales. They first conducted market research to understand their target customers, their needs and preferences. This helped them to first tweak their product so that it would resonate with their customers. This was a lesson for them that customer requirements should drive product design and not the other way round!

Based on the insights gained from market research, Sushil and his team identified the social and web channels where their customers were most active and focused their sales efforts on these channels. They put a CRM in place to automate their sales processes and track their performance. This allowed them to efficiently manage their sales pipeline and quickly identify areas for improvement.

The first thing that they did was to make the software free for the first 3000 customers. They would only pay transaction fees. While they offered a free 7 days trial by default, for these first 3000 customers, it was made free forever.

They also came up with cash backs on achieving certain transaction slabs. This encouraged the initial customers to do more transactions. And since the software was based on machine learning, as more transactions went through the system, the software became more robust and the performance, prediction accuracy, efficiency and user experience improved.

This also gave them some raving reviews which helped to encourage more customers to download the software for a 7 days trial. Most people who downloaded initially did not continue to the paid edition, but the adoption grew steadily as the user experience improved.

Next, they changed their pricing model to suit their customers and created packages based on portfolio size. Initially it was based on an annual fixed subscription fee. They changed it to a combination of a small fixed fee and transaction based charges. This suddenly became much more affordable for customers.

A few months down the line, a few venture capitalists are evaluating them and they seem to be poised to become an unicorn.

Both these stories bring out several facts about sales. As mentioned earlier, sales is fundamental to the business. You must have a strong sales strategy. Marketing can get you leads. But to convert them you need a sales strategy. Various sales strategies exist ranging from promotion schemes, discounts, product bundles, financial structuring, indirect sales, MLM, modern sales channels, etc.

And of course there are complementing marketing strategies. In fact sales and marketing strategies often overlap in certain areas such as targeted promotions. But it completely depends on your product as to what strategy you should adopt.

In the above stories, Richa very smartly used multiple sales channels. Elevating her customers to the level of celebrities was a masterstroke. This propelled her MLM strategy like crazy.

Sushil played around with financial structuring of the sale. He focused on just one sales channel. Since it was a software product, it worked very well for him. But for Richa, just one channel wouldn't have worked. Hers was a fashion product, an aspirational product. People needed to see it and feel it. Physical stores and MLM channels made perfect sense. The E-commerce channel only added to her popularity due to ease of access.

So when you are thinking about your product, you need to think on these lines.

Who is my target customer?

Where is this customer reachable most of the time?

What is the buying behaviour of this customer?

Do I need a few high paying customers or multiple small ticket customers?

How can I make the deal lucrative for the customer without losing revenue myself?

Of course this list can be made much bigger. And you will discover that when you increase this list of questions, it slowly starts overlapping in other functional areas of business such as marketing, product design, logistics, operations etc. And that is but natural because the product or service that you sell is the result of all these functions working together. To be effective in selling, your supporting functions must be aligned with your sales strategies as well.

Too many startups with brilliant products or services fail because of the lack of an effective sales strategy. A lot of time and money is invested in innovation and marketing. But marketing is only effective when there is a sales closure system in place. Unfortunately too less time is invested in planning about faster sales cycles. For most companies it is a quote and negotiation where "negotiation" is synonymous to discounting. Effectively, one ends up leaving too much on the table.

A carefully thought out sales strategy can help you not only to close more sales, but also earn higher profit margin. Besides, such strategies can also provide great inputs for your marketing and operations functions. Sales people observe the actual market from close and if you have trained them well, they can do wonders by spotting trends early enough to create a differentation and help in establish your brand as a thought leader.

CHAPTER EIGHT

Mantra Eight

Have A Customer Delight Strategy

Everyone knows the value of customer service. We have all heard of all the things that one must do to keep a customer happy. And yet, often we see many companies treat customer service as essential, but more out of compulsion rather than genuine intent. This happens because it costs money to deliver customer service. Whether the quality is good or poor, it still costs to provide service.

And customer service is usually provided when there is a problem and the customer is irate. Facing irate customers is not always an experience that a service guy looks forward to. Also, fixing an issue is not always a smooth process. If things go well, all is fine and the customer may get in a forgiving mode. But if the issue is complicated and the service guy is not able to fix it, it only adds to the anxiety in the air.

And that's exactly why customer experiences are not so great when they face problems with a product or a service. You see many testimonials from customers happy with a product. But testimonials about great grievance handling are rare.

But many companies leverage customer service as a sales tool. The moment you decide to think about it in this fashion, the entire picture changes. A customer service event is a great time to interact with the customer face to face! And if you know how to use this time with the customer, you can end up with a great business boost.

Here are some stories to illustrate the point.

I know a small business owner named Maria. She is an online retailer of artistic candles. Now this is a relatively service free product except for replacing broken candles. People buy candles, light them and that's the end of the story. There is very little scope to add a service element here. However Maria wanted to create a differential position for herself and she chose to use customer delight as a vehicle to driving more sales.

Maria made it a point to respond personally to every customer inquiry and comment on social media. Every time there was a broken candle replacement request, she not only sent the replacement promptly, but she sent it with a hand written note apologising for the inconvenience. In addition, she gave a discount coupon as compensation for the customer inconvenience.

She came up with interactive forms for seeking customer feedback and a wish list about what they wanted in their candles. For every great suggestion, she sent a handwritten thanking note and a 100% discount coupon redeemable for the specific product when it became available.

Apart from that Maria offered early access to new products to all existing customers. By doing so, she was able to build a strong community of loyal customers who felt valued and appreciated. These customers not only continued to make purchases, but also shared their positive experiences with others, resulting in increased sales.

Maria used customer service as a core sales strategy because it helped her build trust and rapport with its customers. By showing that she was genuinely interested in not just meeting the customer's needs but also to give them an elevated experience, she was able to differentiate herself from competitors and build strong emotional connections with her customers.

Obviously this approach was more effective than product advertising would have. It allowed customers to experience the brand firsthand, rather than just a promise about a great experience.

In another instance, Payal ran a tiffin service for working people. She had about 200 regular customers and she was fully occupied. There was no possibility of increasing the business due to several constraints such as space, availability of good cooks and chefs, consistency of taste with increased volumes, etc.

As her cost of operations kept creeping up, she had no choice but to increase her prices proportionately. While customers did not object to that because of the great taste and food quality, Payal knew that it wasn't very reassuring. She had a loyal base purely due to the quality of her food services. But beyond a point price would always matter. That set her thinking.

She noticed that she had been regularly getting requests for recipes for certain items that she served in her tiffings. This led her to realise that while people did take her tiffins for lunch, they still cooked meals at home and there was a latent need for help in home cooking. She decided to run a small study.

She personally visited each of her customers over the next few months and interacted with them. She came to know about their dietary habits and individual preferences. She also realised that home cooking was an emotional need for the women of the house despite the fact that they were also working. Most Indian women have it ingrained within their DNA to cook and serve as a token of love and caring for their families.

Cooking is often an elaborate affair in India. There is a lot of preparatory readiness. The actual cooking takes less time, but the prep time takes up a big chunk. A typical wholesome meal takes anywhere between 2 to 3 hours to cook including the prep time. For working women this was a challenge and hence they often resorted to ready mixes, dining out or ordering online. This left an emotional vacuum for them.

She came up with a brilliant plan. She made customised meal kits for her customers. These kits consisted of all the fresh ingredients made ready for cooking. So the lady of the house could now save almost whole of the prep time and get a hot meal ready within under an hour!

The customisation was done based on their dietary preferences and medical recommendations. Payal came up with a weekly planner which she shared with her customers. Based on the plan, Payal would procure the ingredients, pre-cook/pre-mix them and get them ready to the penultimate state. This also delivered a great quality consistency, taste and economies of scale.

These customised meal kits eventually became a much bigger business for her. Today, while she retains her tiffin business and keeps serving about 200 tiffins a day, the meal kit business serves to almost about 1000 customers daily.

The case above is actually about a new product development. However, it emerged out of a genuine effort to delight the customer. Customer centricity often helps to redefine your business. Being close to the customer helps to uncover their latent needs which often have no hope of fulfilment. Such needs getting addressed result in delight. It is way ahead of customer satisfaction.

Both the above stories were from a B2C business. Here is one more from the B2B side.

Mohit ran a software applications development company. He had a few mobile and web based apps for some specific use cases. He had a dedicated services team for handling any trouble tickets raised by his customers. By and large his customers were happy. But Mohit was always worried about competitors capturing his clients. He wanted to create a value proposition that would increase customer loyalty.

So he launched a proactive annual software security auditing service for his customers absolutely free of charge. He would audit all the applications within the customer's environment for security lapses. The holes found within his own applications would be fixed free of charge and those found in the other applications would be explained to the client. They could get it fixed from the OEM or they could engage Mohit's services.

The service was a great hit. The proactive auditing demonstrated Mohit's eagerness to serve his customer better. Free audit showed his commitment to the customer. And the willingness to fix the security aspects for free also underlined his product quality.

The result was that Mohit's software became more and more robust over a period of time. The number of service tickets were reduced and that saved him a big amount of money. Apart from that a few customers requested him to help patch up 3rd party applications which opened up a new business channel for him. Most of the customers asked him to conduct the audit more frequently at a cost.

Application Security Auditing became a separate business vertical for him very soon. This also helped him to get more new customers and built a solid relationship with all of them. The best part was that during these application audits, Mohit and his team could spend a lot of quality time with the customer wherein they could understand the customer's future plans, develop some prototypes proactively and showcase them for future development contracts, and so on.

Again in this example, the desire to delight customers delivered its anticipated benefits. But the outcome was more far reaching than that. Mohit got a whole new line of business which helped him increase his core business as well.

A focus on Customer service turned out to be a pivotal sales strategy because it helped the company create a positive brand image and generate word-of-mouth referrals. By delighting customers, Mohit and his team were able to show tangible benefits and positive experiences that customers were eager to share with others. Mohit's sales pitch automatically went beyond just promoting the features and benefits of his apps!

So when you are thinking about your business, do not stop at the business idea and how great your offering would be. Think about ways in which you can surprise customers. Everyone loves pleasant surprises. Think about all the ways in which you can delight your customers.

For discovering these avenues of customer delight, you can ask yourself a few questions.

What could be other pain points of my customer?

What is the potential problem that my product or service can throw up at a customer?

Can I proactively provide these services so that customers never have to log a service call to me?

What will it cost to provide such service? How can I recover this cost?

How can I use the service opportunity for cross selling and upselling?

Depending on your business, these questions may be tweaked. But essentially, if you have customer delight at a core of your business strategy, it can work wonders for you. Service will no longer be a cost centre, but turn into a profit centre for you!

CHAPTER NINE

Mantra Nine

Draw Your Innovation Road Map

Most startups are very innovative in the beginning. In fact the business is built upon a new idea. The problem occurs when the business starts growing. The innovators now get involved in the daily nuances of running the business and innovation takes a back seat.

Also, generally innovators are not great at execution.

But the good part is that everyone can be an innovator. Innovation can be ingrained in the corporate DNA. It takes a lot of conscious effort and a considerable amount of time. But once the company embraces innovation as a business process, there is no looking back.

I worked with Venky a few years ago. Venky had a software product related to project management. The market for project management was already crowded with many competing solutions and some of them were from very big brands. Venky had a sweet spot beautifully balanced between cost and product features.

But it was a short-lived advantage. Rival companies were constantly launching new features, and Venky and his team were struggling to keep up. They knew they had to innovate quickly to stay ahead.

So Venky and his founding partners huddled together to make a list of features that could set them distinctly apart from the competition. They called this team "The Think Tank". They worked tirelessly for weeks, but every idea they came up with had already been implemented by one of the rival companies. The team was demoralised, and Venky was starting to worry that they would soon become irrelevant or just another run of the mill companies.

The Think Tank was simply not able to deliver. They had perhaps reached their limits of thinking. Or they were thinking within the same old framework. This realisation turned the tables for them. The Think Tank was dismantled and the entire company became a group of innovators. They made an idea wall where everyone in the company was encouraged to pin up a wish list of what their product should be able to do or should stop doing. The wish could be as crazy as it may seem.

That's when one of the junior engineers pinned up a note saying that the projects should be managed by robots. Humans should simply follow orders given by the robot manager!

This wild and outrageous thought was actually picked up and transformed into a feature using artificial intelligence to recommend tasks to users based on their past work patterns. The idea was revolutionary, and the team got to work right away. They encountered numerous challenges along the way, including data privacy concerns and the need to train the AI algorithm with vast amounts of data. But they persevered, and finally, the feature was ready for launch.

The response was overwhelming. Customers loved the new avatar and suddenly everyone wanted to have Venky's product. Venky's sales team cracked many new accounts and captured market share far beyond their expectations.

Today this idea wall is the most visited place by the top management and it is full of new ideas waiting to be picked up and implemented!

This is a classic example of not just product innovation but also innovating the process of innovation. Innovation need not always be product centric. Here is one more story that brings out innovation in a different way.

Eco friendly companies have always been my favourites. So when Radha came to me with her problem statement, I was more than thrilled. Radha's company was into the sustainable products market. They make a highly durable material from non recyclable or difficult to recycle materials such as multilayered packaging, bakelite, ceramic etc. It was specifically useful for furniture manufacturers and other civil construction projects.

Initially the company was doing quite well. But as volumes increased, they started facing delivery problems. They could not meet the demand so customers started going back to traditional materials. Also, their unit economics of production were quite high. That also made it difficult to compete. Clearly, Radha was struggling.

When we looked deeper into the situation, the erratic supply chain was found to be the culprit. The challenge was to collect these non recyclables. Most scrap dealers did not deal in these materials because it did not have any great demand. Stocking a low value item of no demand did not make any business sense for them. So we decided to turn the model around.

Radha pulled up her socks and started talking to rag pickers at the very end of the value chain. She promised them to buy as much material as they could get without any question at a fixed per kg rate. She even went a step ahead by encouraging them to join together in groups and register themselves as a self help group. Radha's company would then provide interest free micro finance to each SHG for such collection.

This dramatically changed the equations. The rag pickers who were earlier not picking up this scrap started scavenging specially for it. Because of the SHG and the financing arrangements, they also started proactively going door to door for collecting such type of scrap. The supply chain became miraculously predictable and the unit cost of procurement went down.

The next challenge was to develop the technology and machinery to handle larger volumes to bring in economies of scale. Bank finance was difficult to get because she had no collateral to offer. Radha approached a few companies with CSR funds dedicated to the environmental cause and convinced them to fund her project. In return, she would proudly advertise their companies in all possible channels including the product branding, collector uniforms, collection vehicles etc.

They got the funds but quickly realised that scaling their existing technology would be challenging. They had to go back to the drawing board and reinvent a new technology that would not just scale up in volume but also adapt to increase the scope of production. They called it the new beginning.

Radha went back to her old customers with a guarantee of supply at a new lower price which they were more than willing to accept. As the word spread about this new material and its benefits, large furniture makers and construction houses made a beeline to her office. Today, within 18 months of the new beginning, Radha's production capacity is full and she is already looking for further expansion options.

In this case, the innovation was in the collection process. Getting the rag picker community together, organising them into self help groups and further enabling these groups with micro finance was clearly the winning formula. The technical process innovation was the second part of the reinvention of the company.

There are many such well known stories of innovation in various areas. Product innovation is often easily visible and therefore most celebrated. But an innovative product often demands a different market segment, a different way of marketing and selling, tweaking your supply chain, reorganising your finances, etc.

Each of these changes need innovative thinking. And you need to keep doing it over and over. Companies must develop a culture of innovation. Every person in the company must be encouraged to innovate. Sometimes, things as simple as reorganising the sitting positions of employees result in amazing productivity enhancements! This is especially true for companies where there are a lot of collaborative efforts.

There are cases of innovative packaging which resulted in a sudden growth in sales of the product. Some examples of this are Snapple and Paper Boat. They changed the beverage industry's packing standards!

Amazon, Flipkart etc are classic examples of success through innovation in the supply chain. Uber, AirBNB are examples of innovation in the way of doing business. In fact they created a new business of service aggregation.

Netflix is an example of innovation in the content delivery process. The entire OTT content industry came into existence and prominence due to Netflix.

All of these companies have developed a culture of innovation. 3M is often quoted as the company with the most exemplary innovation culture. They encourage people to come up with new innovative projects and work on them. All of these projects are fully funded by the company. Of course, there is a timeline and a budget and an elaborate approval process. So beyond a point many ideas die a natural death. Some survive and make it big. Nevertheless, it is a great place for innovators to work.

Ideally tech startup founders, who are usually innovators, should lead the innovation. They should leave the business execution to others. Often, for a startup it is a challenge to get good managers. The best way is to team up. Ideally if you are thinking about your own startup and you have a brilliant idea, you should try to get a founding partner who is good at execution. You can also decide to outsource many things to shared service providers. This will allow you to focus on continuous innovation.

While the initial innovation will allow you to have a first mover advantage, competition will soon catch up. You need to continuously innovate to keep that lead over competition. Else you can perish in no time. There are enough examples of large companies who were way ahead of their times, rather creators of an entire new industry, but eventually languished. The only thing that went wrong was that they did not innovate, and when they did, it was already too late.

So innovation is not something that you do when you get stuck. You need to be at it from day one. The day you have a new idea, remember, it is ready to be stolen. Or someone else is already thinking about something better. So while you need to put to use and monetize your new idea, you simultaneously need to start looking for a new one!

So here are a few questions you may want to ask yourself -

How unique is my idea? How easy is it to copy?

How much time window do I have before someone else copies or betters my idea?

Where all are the areas for improvement in this idea?

In which supporting areas can I innovate to take this idea to the next level?

How will I get constant inspiration for new ideas?

And do not wait till you get these answers. Remember a Version 0 is better than no version at all. Start with a minimum viable product based on your idea. Keep improving it. Google did the same thing. Apple did the same. In fact they keep doing it even today.

So you can do it too. Just get your business idea up and running. Keep refining it and all other supporting elements around the business and you will have a culture of innovation grow around you!

CHAPTER TEN

Mantra Ten

Be On The Right Side Of The Law

I know a lot of businesses that closed down because they violated the law, and I am sure you know them too. Most legal issues happen due to intended financial frauds. But there are others that get into different kinds of legal trouble.

Here are some cases.

Sudhir and Shreyas started a private limited company. Their business was simple. They bought rundown houses, restored them and put them on a timeshare holiday program. They could later sell the asset when they got a valuation multiple times their acquisition price Though capital intensive, it was a very profitable business in the long run.

Since Shreyas and Sudhir had limited capital of their own, they needed additional capital for asset acquisitions and restoration in their early stages. Bank loans would cater to just the asset acquisition. But restoration also needed substantial amounts. And they needed still more capital to grow the business fast. They could not wait for each asset to the restored and then wait for it to make money over the next few years.

So they borrowed some big-time money from their friends Kiran and Manoj. The deal was done based on a mutual understanding of returning the money within 1 year at an annual interest of 10%.

In the following year, they returned some of the principal amount. But asked for some more time for paying the interest. The rest of the principal was carried forward on mutual agreement for 3 more years at the same interest rate. Since it was all on a mutual understanding to date, Kiran and Manoj asked for promissory notes which Shreyas and Sudhir gave.

For some reason, Manoj needed some money urgently for executing a trade in a short time window. So he approached his bank for a short term loan against his promissory note. It so happened that this promissory note was drafted by Shreyas and Sudhir themselves and hence there were many loopholes in it. Due to the ambiguous use of words, the bank decided to probe a bit further.

That's when it came to the fore that Shreyas and Sudhir raised money for their company in a legally incorrect manner. As a private limited company, they were only supposed to take institutional loans or loans from shareholders of the company. Manoj and Kiran did not classify in either category.

The bank could not accept the promissory note. Manoj lost his business opportunity. Shreyas and Sudhir had to undergo some tedious process to regularise the financial transactions which cost a good chunk of money in legal consulting fees and some penalties.

Now, in this case, there was no criminal intent. Neither was there any dispute. And since the dealings were all done within known people, the whole thing got settled eventually. But the point is that it was a completely illegal way of raising money for a private limited company. Had it blown up, it could have caused a lot of embarrassment and perhaps legal penalty for many people.

In one another case, Mr Singh decided to set up a rubber recycling company. He went ahead and acquired a piece of land far away from residential areas, invested in machinery and started his business. Over a period of time, his business grew and so did the residential area which slowly approached closer to Mr Singh's factory.

One fine day a squad of environmental officers visited Mr Singh's plant and locked it up.

Some residents had complained about the emissions from Mr Singh's plant late in the night. It came to light that Mr Singh had initially installed the required emission control systems for environmental compliance. But the scrubbing systems had stopped working long ago. Since the plant was located away from residential areas and no one had objected and considering the cost of repairs, Mr Singh decided to postpone it for a while and asked his supervisor to continue the operations as usual and remind him a year later.

The supervisor changed jobs and no one reminded Mr Singh. Eventually letting the emissions escape without undergoing a cleaning process became the way of life in the company.

When questioned, Mr Singh claimed innocence saying he had no knowledge of the malfunctioned emission control system. The situation got aggravated when Mr Singh tried to bribe the officials. It so happened that one of the plaintiffs was associated with the anti-corruption bureau.

Mr Singh had to spend some time in prison before getting bail. A heavy penalty was charged to the company and Mr Singh had to pay a significant amount as compensation to the residents. All this took a financial toll on the company which soon had to be declared bankrupt.

There are three important points that this story brings out.

One, it is not enough to ensure compliance at the beginning stage. You need to adhere to compliances throughout the lifetime of the business. This happens many times. Initially, to be able to get the required permissions for the business, the businessmen adhere to the regulatory requirements. But reluctant compliance is simply that. It is reluctant. At the slightest opportunity to come out of it, people will jump out of line. Sometimes it may be even by a genuine mistake. But eventually, it becomes a wrong standard. Just like what happened in Mr Singh's case.

Two, ignorance of the compliance gaps, even if it is a genuine ignorance does not mean that you are allowed to breach the law. Compliance is a basic requirement of a business. Laws are made for the general common good. If you breach the boundaries of the law, whether it is by design or by ignorance, it still is against the general good of people. In other words, it is a crime against them.

And three, trying the wriggle your way out of a breach of law through something like bribing is pure blasphemy. Never ever should one do it. In this case, Mr Singh got super unlucky that one of the plaintiffs was from the anti-corruption bureau. Nevertheless, spreading corruption irrespective of your chances of getting caught is still a crime. At some point in time, it will come back to you. I may sound spiritual when I say that the law of karma works. But, as far as legality, morality and ethics are concerned it is often true.

You may get away a few times after breaking the law and bribing your way out. But eventually, all the costs including financial costs, mental tensions, the side effects etc, turn out to be very expensive in many ways. It all comes back to bite you.

In yet another case, a friend of mine got in quite some trouble. He ran a multi-brand luxury automobile showroom. And in one of the festive seasons, he ran a digital marketing campaign on social media. But he made a blunder. He put the specifications of a car model against another brand's equivalent model. It was a genuinely unintentional mistake.

In a day, he got calls from both the carmakers asking him to withdraw the post immediately. He did apologise and withdrew it instantly. But there was a lot of questioning for unauthorized brand infringements, breach of branding agreements and misrepresentation. He had a tough time ironing out the issues.

The point is that even if some things look very trivial to us, they can blow up into serious situations. This story shows that it is not just the government regulations that one has to comply with. You also need to keep in mind your legal obligations to your business partners, customers, and others.

There are many such stories about unintentional trivial lapses as well as big frauds.

You have anti-money laundering laws, anti-monopoly laws, patents and IP laws, copyrights and trademark laws, foreign exchange regulations, labour laws, contract laws, environmental laws, and so on. The list is precociously long. It's almost scary.

And yet, you need to comply with all these. Now as a startup, you really do not have any time to think about this seemingly small stuff. An entrepreneur has a lot on his or her mind. You could certainly do without the additional burden of knowing all the laws and ensuring compliance. It is easier to hire an external consultant.

It is definitely expensive, but the damages liability can literally wipe out your business, just like what happened in Mr SIngh's case. Had he invested some money in restoring the scrubbing system in time, it would have turned out much more affordable in the long run.

In almost every breach of law other than non-financial frauds, the reason is either negligence, ignorance or stupid mistakes. All of it is avoidable with a good legal counsellor by your side.

Having said that, most highly successful businesses tread on the borderline of the law, stretching it as far as they can, often bending it. That is where the money lies. But they take care to not cross the line. Of course, I do not advocate bending the law or ducking under the radar. It is much better, easier and many times cheaper to keep within the boundaries of the law.

But it always helps to know the law well. And even better if you know its loopholes. Not to take advantage of these loopholes, but to ensure that you don't get into trouble if someone else uses those gaps against you.

So ask your legal consultant these questions when you get into a business.

What all laws and regulations are applicable to my business?

Am I compliant with all of them?

What needs to be done to meet my compliances?

What control systems do I have to ensure that others in the company do not break the law?

What kind of SOPs can I create for remedial measures in case someone accidentally breaks a law?

Staying on the right side of the law ensures long terms survival of the business. It may sound like a waste of time and money to many. But it is like preventive medicine. It makes your organization strong from within. A highly legally compliant business will also attract good valuations. There are no two things about it.

CHAPTER ELEVEN

Mantra Eleven

Have A "Plan B" In Your Backpocket

Around the later half of 2018, I was working alongside a group of aspiring entrepreneurs. These were all professionals with decent experience in travel, tourism and hospitality.

Anshuman was a techie. He had worked on the back end technology framework of a few large travel players. He had accumulated quite an in-depth knowledge about how multiple platforms work and what were the pros and cons of each one.

Riya was from marketing. She had worked at several places including a stint at an international hospitality company with both luxury and economy offerings and a few earlier jobs in adventure tourism and theme vacations. She understood the pulse of customers across different socio-economic profiles very well.

Shubhra was from a well known time share holiday company and she brought in immense knowledge about how the industry really worked.

Badri was from a leading travel company and he had access to a great network of alliances.

Now they wanted to launch a tech platform for launching an aggregation service for the travel and tourism sector. Though it was a highly competitive sector, they had some unique value propositions. It was a very interesting and very promising project.

The four of them bootstrapped the startup. They worked out of a rented run-down office in order to keep their costs low. They all decided to take home only as much was barely needed for them to survive. But they did not compromise on the quality of the people. They hired some really talented developers and paid them a handsome salary.

There was no compromise on the development infrastructure. Anshuman and the team balanced their needs for data and IP security, ease of collaborative development, lowering the stress of peering into screens for long hours, ensuring comfort through ergonomically designed furniture, lowest real estate on the desk and importantly, keeping the cost low.

The development environment was hosted on a few servers internally on their common physical network and the developer used thin clients with large 19" screens. Internet access was through a carefully configured firewall and very strict access rules. It was a great setup that made everyone happy at work.

Anshuman was a very hardworking CEO and technically very strong. He led the product development very well and Badri and Shubhra provided the team with a lot of domain knowledge which enabled them to deliver a very impressive prototype well in advance of the deadline.

The investors were impressed with the prototype and Riya's amazing pitch and committed substantial funding for phase 1 of the product. Phase 1 was supposed to last for 3 years and included rolling out the beta version, followed by the final commercial product and acquiring a critical mass of initial subscribers.

The first tranche of investment came in soon enough to the delight of the team.

And then disaster struck. The Covid-19 pandemic was declared and the world went into a lockdown mode. No one could come to work and it seemed that the project deadlines will be missed by a mile leading to big financial overruns.

But Anshuman was not easily beaten down. He gathered himself up and proclaimed that come what may, the development will continue. Over 3 days they put together a collaborative environment so that all developers could work from home. It was tough for a few days but within a couple of weeks, the team was working just as efficiently as before.

But the real problem was not that. The pandemic made the travel and tourism sector its first victim. The entire travel industry came to a grinding halt. No one wanted to travel anywhere anymore. There were just no takers for the product. Phase 1 of getting people on board, pilot testing, and attracting customers to build momentum around the platform started looking like a pipedream.

The founders were completely stunned by the turn of events. Neither the founding team nor the investors nor I as an advisor had a clue about what this whole thing was and how long it could last. All sorts of predictions made rounds and no one knew what to believe. The whole upbeat atmosphere turned grim overnight.

When we all struggled to get our way out, the question of plan B came up. There was no plan B. Anshuman and his team did not believe in plan B. I remembered asking them about it during one of our initial meetings. Riya had said that they did not want a plan B because if something were to go south, instead of fighting their way out, they may be tempted to choose the escape route. That would perhaps be akin to running away from a battle even before it had begun.

It sounded like a brave thought at that time. But in the face of the Covid lockdown, it seemed we needed a plan B after all.

We worked our way out and the company came out with flying colours despite the pandemic. But that's a story for another time.

So the point is that disasters happen. It is Murphy's law. Anything that can go wrong will go wrong. And most of the time it goes wrong at the least opportune moment. It is like when you are crossing a stream with heavy loads in both hands, that your nose starts to itch!

There are several things that can go wrong in a business. Many of these things are internal and the rest are external to the organisation. On most internal things, one can establish a reasonable amount of control through proper planning and a systems-based approach.

Internal factors could range from anything like a fallout between the initial promoters, incorrect investment decisions, wrong execution of a great marketing strategy, low performance, breach in quality control systems, IT infrastructure failure, accidental data loss, intentional data theft, employee attrition, and so on. Like we just said, Murphy's law applies. Any of the above things and others beyond the list can go wrong.

That's where the role of control systems is. Carefully planned management control systems can help in not just mitigating such failures, but also for a smooth way out of any such situations. You need to clearly document the entire workflow, the dependencies, the influencing factors, the monitoring points, measurement metrics, methods of measurement, corrective actions, etc. This needs to be done for each process in each department of the business.

But this exercise takes a lot of time. Unfortunately, entrepreneurs are in a rush to start, and for very good reasons. Also, initially, there aren't any departments in most cases. Almost all the members of the founding team are multi-taskers. A lot many functions do not even exist in the beginning but emerge later. Therefore, most startup ventures have no such carefully planned control systems in place.

This is exactly where consultants can help. Putting in a system is much easier, cheaper and beneficial at the starting stage rather than implementing such structures later. Change management at a later date is a tedious, expensive and often a traumatic experience for the initial team including both the founders and the staff.

In Anshuman's story, it was clearly an external issue that created the crisis. But external factors also trigger internal failures. In this case, there were software development teams who depended on each other and worked in a very strong collaborative environment. With the lockdown being enforced, the infrastructure suddenly became redundant because of non-accessibility.

Work from home was not possible without addressing the security concerns. And it was not possible to simply carry their devices home since they were thin clients. They needed a fat backend server to work on. The developers could not even use their own computers at home. It became an IT infrastructure failure. But thanks to technological maturity and awareness, the team was able to get back on track within 3 days by moving their servers to a data centre and enabling VPN access to everyone.

The collaborative environment was destroyed. So a system had to be set up for collaborative work. A whole new work style had to be created. And there were softer concerns to take care of as well. The whole thing stole a couple of weeks from the development schedule. Had a system been in place for ensuring business continuity in the face of disasters, this time loss could have been saved to some extent.

External factors cannot be controlled. You can only create resilience within your organisation, your systems, your people. A surefire way of inducing such resilience is through the attitude of the leadership.

In the above story, Anshuman showed a great example of resilience. He did not allow his team to develop negative emotions in face of a calamity. Instead, he swung into action and made bold, inspiring statements to the team. Both through words and actions!

He did ensure that the work continued and despite the changed conditions, the team could work smoothly. But he did not have a plan on the revenue side. That could cost him quite a bit. The pandemic destroyed his target market. It would bounce back. But when?

No one had an answer. What should be done? Should you continue pursuing the development in the same direction? Could the development objective be reset? Will it mean a change in business plans? Would existing investors be interested in the changed business model? What if they pulled the plug on further investments?

But since he had an incredible team and very supportive investors, he had some cushion of time. The whole team took the correct advantage of this rare luxury of time and the continued financial support to think through and work out a completely different plan. Adopting the new business model not only kept the company afloat but also propelled it towards brilliant success.

And this time, they included risk mitigation plans for the changed business model. So here is what you could emulate from the success of Anshuman and his team.-

Know your strengths.

Keep in mind alternative business models, should your main one fail or face a crisis.

For each of these models, have clear documented SOPs and have clear monitoring and measurement metrics along with a very effective feedback control system.

List down all the possibilities of risks - both internal and external

Make a clear risk mitigations plan

And do not be afraid of changing over to your plan B. It may lead you to a different destination. But perhaps it may be better than the one that you originally planned for!

Mantra Twelve

Be Sustainable, Be Inclusive

Most readers may opine that this may not be relevant to every business. Trust me, it is. The world is talking about green, climate change, circular economy, inclusiveness, social justice, climate justice and all such jargons. Many companies use these terminologies for green washing. But that is not what I intend to suggest for your business.

Today, sustainability and social responsibility are no longer optional. They are essential elements of a successful business strategy. For startups like, there is an incredible opportunity to embed these principles into the DNA of our ventures, setting ourselves apart in a competitive market. It is much more difficult for an existing corporate giant to pivot around and start doing the green stuff. That's where the advantage of being a nimble footed startup is.

I do not mean to say that established businesses cannot do it. They definitely can, just that it takes substantial dedication of time and capital away from their traditional core and then integrate it within their operations in such a way that it becomes deeply embedded within the company culture. It is much easier for a startup to inculcate sustainability and inclusiveness thinking right from the beginning.

About a year and half ago, I met Meera - an amazingly energetic lady at one of the environmental and circular economy conferences. She hailed from a village near Leh and had won a seat at a very prestigious engineering college purely through merit. Her exposure to the city, engineering hostel life, academic knowledge and her burning desire to uplift people from her community and region were a deadly combination.

Her parents weaved Pashmina shawls for a living and sold them through a local dealer like most of the other village craftsmen. But the younger generation was more ambitious and wanted more. They did not want to bend over their looms for the rest of their lives and be at the mercy of the traders. Many just left homes to seek better alternatives, but seldom got any because of lack of skills and knowledge. The majority of them took up mundane jobs that could barely support them, and yet could not go back because they had not mastered any weaving skills. It was a sad situation and Meera felt that she had to do something for this industry, else it would die. That would be a great cultural loss.

I just mentioned to Meera that she should have a look at companies such as Fab India, Mitti Cool and see what she could come up with. That one line was good enough for her. Today, she has built a phenomenal business.

She reimagined the traditional industry through her newly acquired knowledge and city life exposure. She simply started by introducing organic dyes and a little more organized goat herding practices and projected it as a green product. (Pashmina comes from the Himalayan goat wool). And it was genuinely green. She also organized the artisans into a single entity and started bulk procurement for their supplies. This instantly brought down their costs and increased their profits without increasing the selling price.

The next, she did was introduce solar energy which brought down their operating costs even further. She addressed the capital needs of solar projects through various government schemes and some borrowing from friends. The artisans only paid for the energy used which helped the investors to also make money. The use of solar also added to the "green" product image.

Following that, she decided to look for sustainable packaging. And the story went on as she "greenified" each part of the supply chain one by one. By the end of the year, she had a 100% green product at a lower production cost. With the greenification complete, she is now considering how to create a wow factor before demanding a green premium for the products.

She is thinking of putting together an e-commerce store front with live videos of the entire production process for customers to see. She is also toying with the idea of including block chain technology to trace the entire supply chain so that customers can be 100% sure about the authenticity of the "green" claim and can also trace their purchase to a specific herd of goats if they wished so.

Further, what she has in mind is instead of a fixed price, she would have a base price for the product and a "as much as you would like" green premium that customers may willingly pay for causes such as upkeep of the goats, education of the artisans' children, etc.

I would say that's brilliant thinking. She is achieving multiple objectives here. One, she is making a very strong statement that green products need not be more expensive than normal ones. Two, she is making the customers feel that they have a stake in the entire ecosystem. And three, she is bringing an incredible amount of authenticity to the product by making it traceable right from the goat to the Pashmina shawl delivered at the customer's doorstep.

She is banking on the inherent goodness embedded within every person. Apart from that, many people need to showcase their humanity. Others have a subconscious desire to feel good about helping in a benign cause. I think she may have a huge winner here.

What was traditionally a cottage industry on the verge of dying out, is now transformed into a vibrant brand just by a little different thinking. What Meera did was that she rode the trend of sustainability and inclusiveness. She thought about how she could genuinely make the entire model sustainable and inclusive. Had it been an eye-wash type advertisement as a green product, she may still have been able to sell some goods. But the inherent problems of the industry would still stay. The industry would still die.

There have been other such examples too. Of course, they are all different in their own way. The entire cooperative movement by Amul in Gujarat, the cooperative sugar manufacturing in western Maharashtra, the artisans supply chain organized by Fab India atc are a classic example of inclusiveness.

In another one of the success stories in this book, Radha has created a community of waste pickers for collection. She helped them to create formal self help groups. She financed these groups for collection. The peer pressure ensured that the money was not spent wrongly. And while she could have charged a little interest, she kept it interest free. That is the classic blend of sustainability and inclusiveness.

Another important aspect when thinking about a startup is that your business exists because of your customers who are ultimately human beings. These human beings are all susceptible to the same climate change impacts, the same social unrest impacts, the same economic divide impacts and so on. And therefore, it is super critical that you make sure that these impacts are minimally negative on your customers.

Do you think people will line up at your storefront in the midst of an unsettling thunderstorm or a deluge of rain or at the peak of heatwaves of 50 degree C plus? Do you think a heavily underprivileged, social divide victim will think of buying something from you? Unless you are specifically dealing in such products to reduce their misery, they won't.

People buy in happy times. People buy when their pockets are full. People buy when they feel safe about now and the future. Health makes people happy. A good climate makes people happy. Lesser earning disparities or equal earning opportunities create wealth for more people. People feel safe in the face of certainty. Uncertain climate, uncertain earnings make people feel jittery and they would tend to save for the winter rather than spending or investing in buying your products or services.

It makes perfect sense for any business - startup or otherwise to have a sustainability and inclusiveness strategy embedded in the Company's DNA.

So how do you do it?

The first step would be to understand the SDG goals as stated by the United Nations. There are 17 goals. Choose a max of 3 goals that are most relevant to your business.

To decide what is most relevant, you may have to consider the vulnerabilities of your customers, your employees and your entire supply chain. Based on the vulnerabilities - environmental, social, economic, choose the goals that make most sense.

Once these goals are chosen, think about how you can integrate actions needed for these goals in your entire business process. For example, in the case of Radha, she chose to address the economic and social vulnerability. She organized her supply chain into self help groups thereby giving them a definite identity. She supplied them uniforms that gave them a sense of belonging and therefore safety. She supplied them with microfinance that gave them a definite economic safety net and set a target to achieve.

Similar steps were taken by Mitti Cool, Amul, Fab India and others. Many global brands such as Coke, Pepsi, Nike, Tata Steel, etc have such clear strategies. While the media may highlight a lot of "greenwashing" happening across corporate houses, eventually it will be seen through. And it is always better to focus on the positive side of things than the negative ones.

Treat the climate change challenge as an opportunity to reduce cost, create a differentiator, reinvent the traditional standard process, reimagine your material used. Treat the social justice challenge as an opportunity to attract and retain your workforce. Embed all of this in your brand story. This will ensure that you will create a comparative advantage against your peers.

Sustainability and inclusiveness are not just jargon. These have the potential to be the secret sauce in your recipe for success.

CHAPTER THIRTEEN

The Interim Pause

The chapter has been so titled because it is exactly that.

This is an interim pause. These 12 mantras are not the only ones. But these are the ones that will just get you started. There are many other aspects of starting, running and growing an enterprise. So a small 12 chapter book like this is definitely not the last word.

This is just the beginning. Or perhaps we haven't yet even started!

Entrepreneurship is a multi-faceted constantly changing and evolving dynamic act. It is not about an idea or about money or about personal goals. It is much larger than these or any other single aspect.

We have seen business models evolve over time. While some of the business models have been centuries old, we have seen the rise of businesses that simply did not exist a few years ago. Across different business models, across different industries, across different geographies, across different eras, entrepreneurial constructs and the variables impacting those constructs have constantly changed.

However, one single aspect of entrepreneurship that has never changed is the creation of value.

If your business creates value for your customers, it will survive and thrive. If it doesn't, it will die. Simple. Irrespective of how talented you are, how much investment you pump in, how brilliant your business model is, if it does not create value for your customers, it will perish.

So if you are thinking of getting into any business, and you have already internalized the 12 mantras that I have talked about so far, and you are all roaring to get into your entrepreneurial venture, you need to pause here. Pause. Take a deep breath. Reflect.

Are these mantras applicable to you?

Are these the only ones that matter?

What really matters to your business? What is your business model in the first place? What all does it involve? What are the variables influencing your proposed enterprise? What are the factors that influence those variables? And what are the causes that can trigger those factors?

The more you think, the more of these and many other questions will prop up. To address all of them in one small book is impossible.

What I have tried to do here is to give a framework for getting started. And once you start using this framework, your journey will most likely be a little less bumpier.

About The Author

D.B. Prabhu alias Nahoosh was born in 1972 in a then-obscure distant suburb of Mumbai. He spent his childhood in rural areas of western India where he learned at all places other than at school. At the age of 5, he ran away from his vernacular school to study English, a fascination for which he derived from his doctor neighbor. Three years later Nahoosh was penning his first creative expressions in his mother tongue, the same Marathi language that he had escaped from.

He switched on to his official name - Dwarkanath Prabhu - at the age of ten when he moved back to Mumbai from where he completed his schooling. Prabhu later completed his graduation in engineering and post-graduation in public policy and management from IIM Bangalore, arguably one of the best management schools in Asia. During his IIM days, he worked extensively in the field of technological interventions for social change, education, poverty alleviation, and environmental amelioration and published a few papers in peer-reviewed academic journals on the subjects.

Prabhu's career started and flourished in the information technology industry where he worked as a business - technology optimization consultant for more than two decades. He further expanded his horizons by co-founding Respose Waste Management and Research Pvt Ltd, a company dedicated to creating profitable green entrepreneurial ventures.

All the while, his passion for writing kept smothering deep within and surfaced occasionally in the form of short stories, poetry, essays, and blogs, some of which was published under his old temporary pen name Dhruv Foster. He wrote sporadically in English, Marathi and Hindi languages.

Currently, besides being a business mentor for startups, especially in the technology and environmental space, Prabhu writes fiction under his alias Nahoosh and business and entrepreneurial books under his official identity D.B. Prabhu.

Other Books By The Author

Mining Green Gold

It explores 25 distinct business opportunities across 4 different categories of environment centric businesses. It explains each of these businesses with reference to the problem statement, the solution and its market potential. This book will help aspiring entrepreneurs keen on working in the environmental space to select a project of their liking and structure a business around it.

Available on Amazon

Recycle and Grow Rich!

This book is focused purely on helping aspiring entrepreneurs who are exploring the idea of e-waste recycling as a viable business proposition. "Recycle and Grow Rich!" takes you through the process of making a business plan for your e-waste recycling business through an understanding of the prevailing market context, real grass-root constraints and the risks and risk mitigation methods.

Available on Amazon

IQA - Interesting Questions and Answers about Waste Management

This free e-book is a compilation of answers to many questions that the author has been asked from time to time regarding different types of waste management.

Available on https://www.instamojo.com/DeepInfo/